LIKE THE STARRY NIGHT SKY:
SELECTED POEMS

OBINNA CHLEKEZI

Mwanaka Media and Publishing Pvt Ltd,
Chitungwiza Zimbabwe
*
Creativity, Wisdom and Beauty

Publisher: *Mmap*
Mwanaka Media and Publishing Pvt Ltd
24 Svosve Road, Zengeza 1
Chitungwiza Zimbabwe
mwanaka@yahoo.com
mwanaka13@gmail.com
www.africanbookscollective.com/publishers/mwanaka-media-and-publishing
https://facebook.com/MwanakaMediaAndPublishing/

Distributed in and outside N. America by African Books Collective
orders@africanbookscollective.com
www.africanbookscollective.com

ISBN: 978-1-77928-207-1
EAN: 9781779282071

© OBINNA CHLEKEZI 2025

All rights reserved.
No part of this book may be reproduced or transmitted in any form or by any means, mechanical or electronic, including photocopying and recording, or be stored in any information storage or retrieval system, without written permission from the publisher

DISCLAIMER
All views expressed in this publication are those of the author and do not necessarily reflect the views of *Mmap*.

Dedication
for
Chisom Julius Chilekezi (somsom)

Table of Contents

Preface
Like the starry night sky
A change of taste
Sacrificial cock
The Gambia welcomes you
What a cool day in a rural setting
Who did this to Africa?
Moonlight dance
Cry for the beloved country
Carry your sadness well
We are Tuareg men now
Dying, he died
The new dawn has come
LITTLE SPARROW
Morning song
Our care
Stand up with Johnny
Events of life
The African sees now and shivers
Too tired of this virus of death
Chance
Christ birth
December
Old bailey sat and mourned
Our story of the moment
The locomotive
Haiku
Another Day Gone
It is indeed a season of love
We'll enjoy sounds of music
What has become of you, marriage?

An equal world of love
?
Another star gone
Fruits
Papaya
Mango
When we solve problems
Time
Dimly and unwillingly I have to leave
Early year rains
Night rain
Another day of thanksgiving

Today's rain
You stand in my dreams like Kilimanjaro
I closed my eyes
Toxic Union
What a beautiful morning
??
Success
Aging
Child of different world
I walked my way in dream
Your backsteps
Off it goes
Mathematics must be there
The Breeze
The Season
The Ocean
Black Friday deals
Dear brothers
Let's save the earth
Tower of Babel

Ghost
Vaccination is not enough
Just amazingly
???
Vague
Tremble
Primordial time
African woman
The open arm
The year is winding up
A cosy season
The season … droplets of death beads
The coronavirus war
They pay the price for our lives
Remembrance
All in our hands
Good
Movement song
Good morning birds
For love sack
Oge/Time
Flooding
The Wailing Street
Nightingale
Harmattan Dawn
Dawn
Your card arrived
An escape from
Half of the yellow sun
The melt down
Frustrated people
Walking away from bygone of yu
Economic meltdown

For a new dawn
Umunama
Together as sky
Poem of dawn at dawn
Rejection

Preface

Here I am in Banjul again, coming and going. I am falling in love with this small country and its great people. Banjul is cold this season both physically and socially. It is cold socially as we are in the Ramadan season, the Muslim holy month. It is cold outside too; the month of April is a cold month. Yet, it is not cold with nature. My friends, the birds, are out there twitting, and twitting. One of them is twitting Kuku ble kuku, kuku ble kuku ... on and on it goes.

I am enjoying the whole scenario hence I want to put down some of the experiences in poems, as a testimony of this third coming of this land.

Permit me to note that some of the poems in the collection are writing at the peak of most of the cold mornings. If a part of Africa is this cold, one can imagine what Europe will be. This is the reason; I have never gone to any White People embassy to ask for Visa. I love Africa I no go lie.

It is important to note that some of the selected poems have been published elsewhere. The poems dated two years back are either from my earlier collections like Rejection and other poems (2007). Nevertheless, some of these poems had appeared far much earlier in publications like Twenty Nigerian Writers, ANA Review, Daily Times, Rake, etc. The poem 'Nightingale' was read on Radio Nigeria in the 80s in one of their programmes while the poem 'Your Card Arrived' has appeared in ANA Review and some other places.

To my readers and fans, you are there for me and I appreciate you all.

Serrenkunda, The Gambia

Like the starry night sky

Am African
Skin black, like the feathers of crow
My lips brown, deep as the soul
Nose flat, breathe-full and beauty
Above all, am African
Black, beautiful as a starry night sky

A change of taste

This tongue ever used to the palm
Liquid fresh from the backyard tap, whitish
Bubbling in kindness, soothing
Good gift of our goddess Bacchus

Thought I have tasted it all
Till this Saturday, on my dining table
An O' Orla Maritima, Vinho tinto
 Portuguese tapped, 12.5% vol.
Instruction foreign
Proveniente de casta
De excelente sabor e bouquet
Not even a kind word in English

Carton wrapped
Colour red like blood
Taste good while chilled
Inviting, tongue twisting

Colour quite different
Even in taste from our whitish
More powerful than tapster's best
O' Orla, just inviting …

I have begun to fall
Asleep, even too soon …

Sacrificial cock

At the foot
Of the gods
An epicentre
Of the community's
Appeasement
A prime cockerel
Just in its full prime
Humped into the arena
Of this bloodily offertory
O' what an
Additional ingredients
Just from the gods for the gods
To devour

May I
Be not the first to
Journey through
The roads
That the gods
Have been offered
Ingredients for
Appeasement
At dawn
Neither be
A sacrificial cock
That present self
As an add-on to waited
Sacrifice, just
A sacrificial lamb
For the gods
To devour.

The Gambia welcomes you

just at the stepping down off the craft
sweet nightly fresh breeze
blows across, signifying welcome
you move on, seeing the aviary
presence, even in the night

you are driven on the road,
security checks. they salute and
ask you to move on, even in the night
as you step into the hotel, warm smile
fresh like that of tomatoes, awaits
at costly price. things cost much here!
you wonder. someone taps you
'this is a country for tourists'
now I know

the streets clean and peaceful
a baby masquerade walks, dance past you,
with a cutlass, and they say it's blunt, harmless
just for the fun of being a masquerade.
you look across. see cows walking majestically
see donkeys too carrying off the nation's burdens
you try to show some pity for it
you are told its part of the culture

you walk all alone, along the beach
there beautiful damsels showcasing …
even dogs go there to catch fun too
you further stretched and see, pink and pink
flesh, unwrapped, dot the beach, cradled in bikinis
smiling and dancing, some speaking in foreign tongues

see how they spread across, trying to melt their icy skins
others entangle hand in hand with rastas. they say it's
part of the fun, and it goes beyond the beach to some closets

the country welcomes you
in smiles, it's so full of smiles, even in hard times
you meet faithful who cast all burdens to Allah
supplier of all needs. nothing to worry. the country
welcomes you with open hands, expecting same from you
I love this country, its birds, its others
it welcomes all not minding your skin.

This poem was written during my first visit to The Gambia and it mirrors how I have perceived the country right from the airport down to the airport.

What a cool day in a rural setting

the day wakes up gradually with warm smiles
and melodious tweets of birds and of insects
scattered in the cool morning of the day
what a melodious life, of rural life of dreams

oh look, the marigold adorning the roads
flowers wide and beautiful breathing and fresh
on dusty roads of brown dying leaves of the season
oh see too the masquerades gyrating more dusts to be

I stand lost in the season of dreams and flowers
listening to the birds
listening to crickets
I wish my life all to be spent
here, among the season, and of dust and of flowers

what a dream of dreamy desires
what a friendly scene to behold, of
the palms spreading their teeth in the sun
and nights cold as moon
brother, am here not to venture back to the city

This poem was written in Ikeji in Osun with calm life unlike that I daily experience in Lagos

Who did this to Africa?

Listen to the black cries
in the tenements.
Bread! a hand! a smile!
Lanre Peters (Satellites, 1967)

The rain season, it came
Fully dressed off it went. The harmattan
Lashed out and out heat sweat
Pains and hunger across the land
& the farmer mourned the season
The people cried, everyone in tears.

The season is running out
Its calendar, of four plus four
Hope damaged, differed
Youths took to the streets
Endsars end sadness!
Then harvest of blood. Innocent blood!
At the peak of the dreamed change!

Arms up
Faces up
Towards the unknown
Hope differed
Hope rose to unknown god
As we look up to the unknown

This is Africa
Where problems are invented each day
By the leaders for the led.

This is Africa where we manufacture problems
& ask God to solve them, not our portion
To harvest our handmade problems but that of the gods

Maybe the portion of others
Europeans, Americans
Asians – or them all?
We select bad leaders, celebrate them
Call upon God to help us solve problems

Africa my Africa
Who made you this way?
From Cape Town to Cairo
From Lagos to Harare, same cries, same stories
Who did this to us?
Definitely not the ancestors, but who?

* Poem written in Lagos during the endsar riot where young people called for change but the change never came.

Moonlight dance

Son
The moonlight is out
Join us in the dance of the ancestors
Enjoy the price gift of nature, ever limitless
For when you go to sleep
Too earlier than desirable
The night becomes longer
Than the day

For
The night is ours to bask in
As much as a waste of night's fall

Son
Come and relieve your worries and sorrows
In the dance of the moon, as my fathers did
Happy and sing in moonlight of joy
Whisper to the winds while the night slow to dawn
In sweet nightly orchids, so slow to break
And like the ancestors we dance as a family in love

Son
Are you still on bed with your bookish wife
Strange, while the moon laughs in a merry round
Just in some sort of ambles go
And nature entwines as the moon in a laughter share
And the sound of laughter grows stronger, shared by siblings
Mimicking a slow winding stream fall
The moon takes us all by hand for dance
Taking away solitary moments and
Laughter fills the night's fall with joy

My forbearers
Learnt dance steps of love
At the shine of the moon
Who else in the hamlet
That did elsewhere, than in the dance of the moon
Come out and dance in the shine of the moon
For
When you go to sleep
Earlier than desirable
The night ends longer than the day.

© *22/03/2021*

Cry for the beloved country

Cry for the beloved Country
the devil, like a dragon spider, befriended
the ruled, the ruler, the murderer and murdered
as hot bloods split out, spreading on the tiled road
just like a sour dream chugging forth
reminisces of the thirty months, of
red rain in the land, of no learning by all
to both sides of the divide, peace is not
a virtue; as political venom split out
and hatred are; misinformation spread
intolerance order of the clime
spreading, devouring, and another cries
dripping in red and further cries
our nation burns
and this red rain offensive to the sky
this a dream or what
as social tongues cut half the already
dead peace in the land, so more blood split
in this nation, neat clothes torn into pieces of rags
date your dead
date your wounded
what a sad dream to behold.

Published in the Daily Trust of 7th November 2020

Carry your sadness well

Sunday was an eclipse
The darkness overcome the beauty of a day
I saw you boil like a volcano
Unstoppable, the lava purges on and on

I have seen ecstasy of love shine
And bitterness and hatred groom in you
Just like the petal fades from the hibiscus
And the heart spread venom as smile

Come off it, this should be another day of love
As the clouds cannot withhold the rainfall for too long

See the mash, the frozen music of dawn
And the sun spreads the day with laughter

You cannot stand there all alone, along with sadness
Come up now join the world to smile
Each a person, with a burden to carry
And yours not an exception to be.

We are Tuareg men now

this virus turns all
to Tuareg men of Sahara
veiled to the eyes
locked down to our veins

stay home, stay safe, the jingle goes
but the real Tuareg men a nomad
not for the microbe but as their lives
but here we are, locked down and masked

our world ever diseased but not this kind
of stay safe, stay home for nomads
the diurnal species, homo animalized
actively, mainly, during daylight

then the novel corana mask
gift from unseen microbe, turning
our world to that of Tuareg men
all veiled, as they walked in the broad daylight.

13/06/20

Dying, he died

Should we celebrate death
As we do in birth?
For full of fear of days ahead
The newly born child cried and cried;
Cries wasted with the passage of time
In living in the wrong side of life
Showing much hubris to others
While death stares at each of its steps.
As the child bows through the bough of death
Lost in thought, at the entrance of death
Confused, cried for a second chance of birth
Seeing a wasted journey from its birth
It cried for its birth
That end in painful death.

the new dawn has come

this new dawn
of hope and change
let's embrace for keeps
the new dawn has come
our dawn of hope
this dawn by truth
I'll pull down
dirt on our face
    the new dawn has come
    our dawn of hope
so, lets now celebrate
and work for its keep
as never again shall our flag
a symbol of shame be
messed up by greed …
    the new dawn has come
    our dawn of hope
so, let those whose wealth
our collective wealth is, return
in exchange of forgiveness
and collective love reign
    the new dawn has come
    our dawn of hope
yes, the new dawn
early morning birdsongs filled
our dawn to celebrate
    the new dawn has come
    to celebrate for keeps.

What shall we eat today?

our cry, heard across boundaries:
what shall we eat today?

Hunger strikes the land, as
food scarcity flood all across
our market; so brutal and ludicrous, it is
armed with anger and hunger, our youths
exalted moments of shrinking lucidity

We're crying, crying and crying, for
what shall we eat too
as the green grain of her skin
fades, yellowish and *kwashiorkored*
as hunger continues to flood the land

We have lived with much hunger
in a land vast with vegetations, to till
while able young blood waste in dreams
of mirage of white-collared job, nowhere to be seen
while they too cry: what shall we eat today?
this is not the land, our land, we know, in
this fragile non-peaceful co-existence of hunger
and anger at this pointless infantile time, so
filled with cries and cries of: what shall we eat today!

LITTLE SPARROW

My little sparrow bird,
Shaking the twig
 Between the leaves
  On and on, it hops

            On and on to my window it hops
            What's mine its songs?
            On and on it tweets, melodiously
       Little sparrow, mine.

Morning song

    I
Beautiful morning
It is the world that wakes
Up from darkness to light
As our sun smiles in shine
The birds all full of morning songs
The drowsy legs sing too to work

Morning so full of songs
Beautiful morning of songs
To behold indeed!

    II
A stale night so full
Of tales spinning briskly
Into dawn, but with
Half full dreams
At dawn, presenting me
A strange harvest of
Wants, hunger and pains

I plunge, plunging
Into the hazy light
With a willed cavernous
Silence

I move on and on
And on into the day's song.

19/09/2020

Our care

One of us, continually, smiles, walking
All alone, talking to self.

One of us in a troubled world, caring
Less for one another, with one of

Us in a troubled mind, yes one of
Us in dear need of love, care

And not in despite, not rejection
Yes, one of us is in dear need of all us

Yes, to love
And care
For all of us
In a troubled world
And with troubled mind.

Stand up with Johnny

Worries eat the
Day like acid
But can the day
Be saved,
Oh, day of lack
And stolen sun

The moon beacons
With hope, and
Subtle smiles
Stand up with Johnny
For the sun will
Out run today's
Darkness

Events of life

Our mind
Could be overrun by events
That could occur to anyone
Caused by crushing stress
Drowned by fluid pressures
Of lives' demands of existence

Causing sudden stoppage
Of smiles, and ineffective
Workings in our body

Our mind
Are dunces
In some life matters
That ends us in grief
Such as this, to know.

The African sees snow and shivers

The world in a deep freezer, very cold
After days of heat and summer burnt
Here am I an African, I walk, I freeze, I shake but smile
A newcomer knowing that the world needs this cold too
To further live, so that we can live too

I stand here a newcomer to snow, staring at this wintry love

Do I claim to love this cold, not at all, but great love for the grayish sights?
Hope this scene be transported back home but without this killing cold
So my kinsmen too share in this shock of walking in earth's deep freezer too
As here the day walks in a cold smile from dawn to dusk
And the lonely newcomer befriends more loneliness across the streets

I stand here a newcomer to snow, staring at this wintry love

Yes, here the day smiles with a cold smile
The African on strange journey dreams of nothing but home
"Take me home, to Africa, our land of perpetual sunshine"
As the bald-head man walks along the wintry street, receiving strange slaps of snow
"Take me back home, to Africa, to our land where the sun never fails to show its teeth each day"

I stand here a newcomer to snow, staring at this wintry love

Here the weather is a god, especially during winter

Here the weather is part of the daily devotions,
The people draw their timetables of to go or not to go with the weather in mind
Here in this cold weather, a lonely newcomer dreams of his sun
The lonely newcomer shivers as snow falls, buzzing, blowing very ray cold sirens across.

Too tired of this virus of death

this earth in pernicious season
witnessing deaths across
like leaves, dried, falling freely as rain
and behold fork like cries in towns

the virus is closer and swift
and our hare brained people
unaware in this killing denial
hastier leaves continue in falls

and daily multiplication of deaths
brew detestable and malignity
see flowers fade easily, young and old
more shooting stars now in tombs

see again the streets, across this market
urchins rambled unconcerned in haughtiness
and few that knows like waltzers waiting
swing too in this generic dance denial

the hour abate this season of death in our hands
and we stiffen unfeeling falls into the tombs
and inure virus gaiety across
truly, we cry, "fly away and away!"

and when will this life again come back
to its contented robin song again
"Oh, life come back to Life"
mankind is too tired of virus deaths!

We are all brown, colourful
You are not my colour
I am not your colour
And we are colourful,
See you and I in love
Seeing just the brown in between,
As we cannot separate white and black
in our blood

We are just beautiful
You and i
As we are all just brown
Not colour-blind, but *colour beautiful*
When we love one another the more?

10/5/2020

Chance

We blow along with the everyday storm
Not only by chance and not also by our desires
We sail each across life stormy waters
But my chance some in this sail in canoes,
Some others in beauty to behold Yachts

Let all sail and sail by this chance

But who we are, not by chance to be
As not by chance that my worries have their worries too
Leaving me less anxiety to manage
So not my chance do I sail in this nature given canoe
To sail to safety, love and happiness, and
To them that needs my love

Let all sail and sail by this chance

Paddle your Yacht as I paddle my canoe
Let all do same with love, to others
And not my chance we love those who meet our sails
To help those in need of love by our extended arms
So that by tomorrow, our refusal to love
Will not give birth to perilous days for all

Let all sail and sail by divine chance of love!

Christ birth

at this season of snow and cold
a child is born, our Christ is born
to bring us warmth and love, to cherish
and with His love overflowing like a stream;
O' come yea and rejoice for divine manifestation
For Christ is born, His birth our birth indeed.

December

This year that just began
Is dying to an end
With the greens and lushes
And the fresh and clear air
All turning to the dry

It's hot, dry and dusty
A little nightly colder

It is the season of gathering smiles
And seeing people off distances
Yes, we are in the December of
Hearing kin's footsteps now and now

It's weird without the December winds and traffic
Brother, I must go home to break early morning kola
As Christmas can be better celebrated with siblings

Old Bailey sat and mourned

He was part of the process
Harvesting things out of his bare hands
Until the advent of the cursed engine
Steaming out life from man
From dawn to dusk and dusk to dawn

There's no longer rest at sight
As the master with wipe in hand
Push and push the workers
And his God-cursed engine
Preying upon humans for more
And drugged with humbled hurry
Like a stream, sweaters flew and flew
To nourish the master's dream

Old Bailey sat and mournful
Licked his sweater as the engine
Chopped off the finger of a colleague
With broken fingers and bloody sweats
The order of their day
Of a mangled mass
Of labours
Back bent aside by sufferings
From the new great engine

Our story of the moment

yesterday was All Saint's Day
foreshadowing the advent
of this great birth, all the mission
ground with smile
let the guns across the globe
for a moment, and let's
roll out the euphonium for now
his birth, our birth, a euphonious birth
it is

all shout Eureka
for Christ is born, even in a virused world as this

no need for a long epistle, for
we don't need another coming of Magi
for he lives in our house
his epitaph on our soul this season
this our apocalypse
and our story of the moment

This locomotive

This is a locomotive year
with lots and tons of hiccup
all around the journey
from the fresh start
of its first moon to the last twelve;
the journey so full of freights
with its killing flu

and lots of lockdowns across the globe
with, wedge and screw
all threatening and shaky too
we move, not without hope
and wait of the magic wand vaccine
yes, we'll move on to safety
our lives together
as we wait for another year's offerings.

Haiku

My country pants like a lapdog
And signs of slow asthmatic death rattles across
Indeed, there's coronavirus in the land

I plucked this wild rose
Mystical as she gets into my skin
And I am left with scar

The festival has come and gone
But the gods unappeased with our sacrifice
We are here with small-pox-infected blanket

The world milks the cow, so as
To feed its dogs, parrots and cats
That is capitalism

Cancer marked him dead
Then the unbelievable miracle
His sun came up to shine

Another Day Gone

a bright day
to behold, a new dawn of
laughter and faith

do I
need an astrologer
to decode the beam
of laughter on the moon

I have seen
seasons of pain
and known too, pain
and pain too painful to behold

so let me
walk through the backdoor
and steal serum of joy
you give

oh it's another day gone bye
missing smiles of the moon
shine on your face
oh, what a day to behold

It is indeed a season of love

This is not the best of times
But it is the season we are
The darkling season of locked down, a viral season
Hunger grows in homes like fruits on mango tree
It was at this that food stores closed for rear

A mother indoors with children and hunger
As government closed down roads
And mother a pretty trader, and mother of five
Feeding from hand to mouth, day in day out
And the roads blocked, locked down

The children cried and cried, all to high heavens for food
But God's eyes seem not watching them
And the cries blew like noise winds to the neighbourhood
And the neighbours were disturbed, neighbours can't take it further
What's to be done! Let's get the police to end this mess

Not for Jabbar, widowed, like the biblical widow
The pang of the cries touched her soul, she was moved to act
"What can I do?" "What should I do?" she tweeted!
No, it must end, the cries of these God's gifts
She looked up to havens and saw God's eyes watching

That early morning dawn, off she set out
She left out with her most valuable of possession, a gift – precious
"No", she said. "These children more valuable than gold!"
Buy my gold goldsmith for those goods in need!"

Jabbar sold her gold, she sold those valuables
She bought foods, and foods and foods

She thought of the happiness it would give to the children
She looked, saw God watching, and thanked Him for the gift to help life

Jabbar and the police invited by neighbours arrived same time
Police to take away the nuisance, and Jabbar to give gift to God's gift
"Officer leave them", "I will stop the cries" she said
Off she went, off-loading her load of love, with police given lending hands

O' the soulless neighbours, walked away in shame
This happened in this coronavirused season, a season of pain and of death
We in this season that damped the best of humanity from we all
Yes, this coronavirus season is of love and compassion.

We'll enjoy sounds of music

Cheerful thought flows like sounds
Of drums, and winding tales
Happiness flows like the river
It's so beautiful a thing to behold

Yes the sound of music
It will flow and flow
The trumpet, piano and drum
We will celebrate the victories

We'll dance to tom-tom drumming
We 'll celebrate in the post Covid 19 times
We'll hug, hug and laugh to the stars
Yes, we'll enjoy the sound of music too.

What has become of you, marriage?

They say we should just watch with tears
The land had caught cold, and it is frozen
The river is filled up, but with tears
When the heat of this summer turned self-cold
The man leaves his wife, leaving behind his cross of tears
As the wedding ring of their marriage has turned cold
Today's marriages are turning to mirage and rustic tears

An equal world of love

Let the sunshine on all
Not minding their respective gender
For none creates himself or herself the way we are
Why all this noise of he is a man and she a woman,
Of hate and damage and destruction of humanity
When men love women to cherish and to live with
        When we build to be in our midst
        The world a happier place to be
        And where only part of the gender smiles
        The other in the hallow pit of sadness
        A great world has been killed!
So wherever you go and wherever you be
Take up as part of you to uphold
That a world of equal gender, to have, we should
For a world of equal gender is no way less a world of equal smiles
Let the sun shines on all whether with penis or vagina or none at all
So as to have a world of men and women holding hands
Creating a great world of peace and growth for all and for our children
        When we build to be in our midst
        The world a happier place to be
        And where only part of the gender smiles
        The other in the hallow pit of sadness
        A great world has been killed!
The world of equal gender is a world of equal dreams
Let us build this world of our great dream to be
Of equal gender and equal love and we will all feel alright.

When we abuse women
We all, our laughter, too
when we abuse them women?
and reducing humanity to rag

Brother, you see not the rot you cause
knowingly or not, as all dirty rag
when all turn to, that the pride of a woman is lost

The smile and fragrances of a woman
for all to behold and cherish
when we all agree to uphold womanhood

Lets not abusive
so that the world shines out its love

?

a bad day it
was for us all,
father had died,
I was told.
sad and mournful
but the sun of remembrance
shines and shines in my heart
awaken me up
for he had lived a great life.

Another star gone
(for Jerry Agada)

Where do we find another him?
The hawk has stolen another chick of the pen family
Away of no return he has gone, so assembly
The drums, the gongs and flutes, for
Another writer has gone the way of the ancestors

But
Could I ask him
Why!? ...
Death shouldn't have drawn him
Away from us, this soon

Do we mourn him?
Whose dreams will taste not death?
Whose pen will produce successors?
Ever after this horrible year of deaths
And lockdowns

Leaving us another festival of mourning
And of tearful tributes and memorial anthologies
For another literary hero, another star
Has existed the extra-literal constellation
We left with void, of tears, and reminiscence

Adieu Jerry Agada
Write on to eternity
For this Jeremiad may not be enough!

Fruits

Taken as
And for vitamins

They boost our immunes
Keeps us ready to
Defend ourselves against
Diseases and sicknesses.

They that eats fruits
See the doctor less
As they had already

Taken their drugs
Knowing or unknowing

Papaya

Give me papaya
to quench my thirsty;
and increase my immune to virus,
give me papaya, and its
vitamins, O' sweet vitamins
succulence to the tongue.

Oh give me sweet papaya
and equip me to be battle ready
fighting foreign bodies
that could harm my body

Oh, papaya
sweet fruit
great taste
and like the bees to the flower
I crawl to the papaya tree
For its succulence

Mango

Yellow
Succulent
Attractive to
Bees and man

Mango
Sweet fruit
A taste, great
To lick and lust
For, I have not
Seen a sweet fruit
Just as you, O' mango

when we solve problems

when we solve problems
talking to others
than clenched fist of fury

when we solve problems
when we see eye to eye
than this cauldron of hatred

when we solve problems
and see hope and light
in the green white green

a nation great
to build
when we solve problems

as one people

Time

Precious
easy, to
lose

time
unengaged, it
takes up wings
just like a bird
flying away, it does

time transcends, too,
if unengaged to work,
away and away, it flies
beyond and beyond
imagination

engage
your time
preciously
to work, for
its worthy
to do so.

Dimly and unwillingly, I had to leave

"And then she thought, looking about the kitchen: 'Lord, wouldn't it be a blessing if he didn't never come back no more.' The Lord had given her what she said she wanted, as was often, she had found, His bewildering method of answering prayer. Frank never did come back".
James Baldwin's Go Tell It On The Mountain

Eerie cries everywhere everyday
As gray clouds over shade the sun everyday
But looking outside beyond the shade are mine
Invisible tears, hidden but walking about my day
And who will hear my own stories, no need today to tell

Adulterous, yes!
Scorn, tears filled the heart, not my dream
Not what I had dreamt along the moonlight dance
I left, stepping out on mists that covered the ground
With filled regrets and betrayal full too, to unknown

Unlike Lot's wife, no looking back
I move, dimly and unwillingly, leaving behind
Both tears and joy walking out of that hateful room
I left. Never to revisit my vomit!

Early year rains

The heat had had its way
For long time of drought
Agreed, in hot season, we are
Never had it been this hot

The cloud darkens
Hiding the face of the sun
And gentle winds sail across
Leaving a gentle touch on the face

It began to rain …

You cannot imagine
This smile on the faces
Of leaves, under the showers
Of this mighty fall of rain

See the little bird nwanza*
Soaring and dancing in the rain, not alone
The fowls, insects and others all
Taking their first bath of the year.

Is the smallest bird in Igboland where the poet comes from

Night rain

Night falls in rain
As night became darker than usual
Minutes later it rained, bucketful, everywhere, and
The stars ran too into their homes, for fear
Of flashing lightning, with no control
Across the dark face of night

The thunders too at war, roaring and rolling,
This night, unsafe, of moonlight steps
The moon calls of its shine, we call off our dance
For the ground slippery with mist and fear
The rain 'd taken off the moonshine, taken off our moon laughters
Night has fallen in rain, fall in pains.

Another day of thanksgiving

The sun appeared majestically
On my window-pane
With a burning-like silver
Bright, a beauty to behold

The dusk on its way home
Oh the day is past spent

It's been a great day
Of dreams achieved, delayed and wasted too
I look up
Oh another day of thanksgiving is gone.

Today's rain

It came all the way like a thief
Unannounced, slowly and slowly
The sun caught unawares, as it
Continues to bask in gold up there

Today's rain
Came with storms and winds
And rained heavily later, leaving
Behind road micro-rivers along footpaths

Today's rain began slowly
And rained heavily beyond imagination

You stand in my dreams like Kilimanjaro

Another year has begun
And the old one faded away, not to be seen
I only see you in dreams, as we do our dead
I see you in morning dreams, mid-day dreams and night dreams

You are always in my mind
Standing still like Mount Kilimanjaro
I have sought the medicine of the white doctor
To expunge you from me, but
No hope, no help, there you still stand
I have sought the medicine of our witch doctor
To expunge you from me, but
Still no hope, no help, as you stand there still

I have not sought to see your face
Once more, to see if it can kill
This urge to see you again
But there, standing as a river in-between
Is coronavirus, that killer virus
Closer of doors and borders, divider of homes

Soxna, now that a new year has begun
And hope of seeing you still dim with this virus around
As you come to me in dream today
Please untie me, lets wonder away from you
Until we see the end of this virus.

I closed my eyes

Walking out is not an end
Walking out is the beginning
Of more headaches, of lies
Flying about like owls
And new magnetic attractions
From other serpents, all across

I wait, I closed my eyes…

The face of the moon shines
Brighter, it shines more
In heart no bitterness.
I have not seen in the past, you moon
Shines as you shine now

I smile for it's a new dawn
I can see a day again, of sunshine
Less of morning hates
As the sun shines, it shines love for all.

Toxic Union

They say to separate
Is to go to hell fire
And what of living
In a toxic union, they
Remain silent, leaving
One to wonder, whichever way
The pains are better there
Than from here to there

I move, I walk away
I separate myself from the fire
Before the fire reaches there.

What a beautiful morning

Birds' songs hit my eardrum
With sweet melodies
While still on my sleeping mat

And the morning weather
Just like cheese to savour

It rained last night
And the day wake up in freshness
And in melodies, and in new hopes

A beautiful day
It promised to be.

??

you want to cut the creation path
with your matchet when its first cut
of nature is yet to heal, are you
the mad chick that went for a dangerous
safari of swallowing the slippery snake ending up
being swallowed by the veracious snake
the aftermath all against the snake
this world cannot be balanced indeed
little wonder it's spherical and not cyclical

can you imagine this
the day the other day break in bad dream
a perched bird hooked to a branch tip
unconscious of the events of previous night, as
day woke up in further darkness
they said it was because of the coming rain
the trouble of the farmer is not the concern of
the weaver bird weaving nests and nests
at the branches of the iroko tree that hosts the totems
of the family chi*, the rope over the family lake, the
gods that shielded its own during the slavery era and times of war

the weaver bird weaves songs and
songs and songs too that early morning
to the sweet delight of the waking environ
the busy spider, not too far off, weaves alongside
silky traps for innocent flies, thoughtless
dancing in flight to tunes of free songs in the air
there on a sweat-soaked mattress a weakling struggle
in an endless dream of his smoky tomorrow

his own hope: there's a tomorrow, a better one
instead of death let's struggling continues
let the song dance alongside the sun
if the birds of the air are always lucky for food
what else is man, so loved by God
let the birds go on so on in songs
and tomorrow will care for its own
the wills of the gods are like the sun
so far for one to change its direction
who can even fight the gods?
who can even cut again the road of creation with matchet?
he who feeds the birds, will definitely feed man
the beauty of creation**

Chi means personal god in Igbo land and every family before the colonialism had one hoisted before a tree in the family compound among other gods for protection.
*** the Igbo word for man is mma ndu shortened for madu which means beauty of creation*

Success

As
The champagne corks
Popped out
From the bottle
& The liquid sparklingly
Splash across in flow

A mark
Of 'let's celebrate'

Brother
Let's cheers
For the enwombed dream
Safely delivered

A story
Of from the gutters
To the skyscrapers
With fear filled dreams
Walking through the streets.

Aging

Agbomma, you laughed at a man
who had climbed seven mountains?
a day and come down so full of breath.
Age slows but never to destroy a man's
history-in-pocket of events.
You laughed at a man
whose pocket so full of episodes
of crossing seven rivers and still alive.
Aging like a lock padlock, the blood routes.
In chains, the blood like a river
flows reaching all the banks of the body
until when death will in a surprise visit comes.

Agbomma, stop. Stop. Don't tempt.
The old never forgets dance steps
learnt in the prime. So stop.
Don't mind that the bites of the dog
is always strong because of its strong teeth.
And should be feared too. So laugh not the old
For what you are he was and you to be.
Age is just numbers. & The power of Mr. Penis
is not in the size. Stop Agbomma. He who has
no respect for elders knows his ancestors.

This aging strong as the shoe glue. Mr. fox has
lost its tricks. The king lion dying of starvation.
Can't hunt anymore for games. Its prey
Ramba dance before. Even playing with their fingers
Guitar with the tail of the lion. Kinsmen come &
hear my lamentations! The son of the soil can
no longer perform natures duties. He can no longer

obey the command of go and be fruitful. Fill the earth.
Do we blame Agbomma to laugh at him?

No more nature's duty for a failed battery.
Aging comes like a thief in the night.
Unnoticed. Stealing and destroying that
was, once, useful to have and kept for life.
The lion has turned to a lamb & Agbomma is laughing
What an irony?

Can you imagine?
Last night at the village square
Agbomma called me her fellow woman.
Not just at that. She also called me a weakling,
with no smoke at the end of the barrel of my gun.
She laughed and laughed. O' Laughing damsel.
She is that beauty. Just as the early morning sun,
whose beauty rises with the rising sun. Agbomma
the desire of real men. Am just remembering my lost
youthful days. Forget it. Story for another day.
But today here I am. Being laughed at. Being called a woman

Agbomma, she, when being admired, the farmer forgot
to take his hoe to farm. Look now
Agbomma laughed at the village cat, the wrestler whose back
never touched the ground. Who attracts village damsels?
in his youth as bees to their honey. A woman. A weakling.
It's not her fault. It's the fault of growing old. A sack not
to be carried by all until death. Aging irreversible. The thread
that ties the muscles together, in chain and in pain.

Agbomma, you have turned to a tsetse fly
Perching comfortably, unconcerned, on my scrotum.

Confused I am. Either to hit and hurt myself or
let you continue to enjoy your laughter.
Princess, don't much more. Don't
push me too further. Don't. The old man be forced to
retrace his steps in remembrance of forgotten dance step.

Child of different world

I am bound by blood to this land
its air, rivers and songs haunt me
my umbilical cord lies cold, decayed, underneath it
a giant palm tree marking its spot
it, the link between my ancestors and me
in unbreakable tethers.

The bivalve form of me
child of two different world
with that single line as a hinge in the middle,
the gods and this land beacons its worshipper
but the gory of the other world tightly holds
my land had been visiting me in dreams, lately
the aroma of its stew tempting me back
then the visual interruption, a barrier at the midpoint
"Love – for another person, a place, the self –
requires we wrestle with our imitations"

I am bound by blood to my land, my heart
and lungs all longing for its grace and calm
but the city glows with laughter, though no sweetness
the city steals its own for keep, flashy lights here and there
making one lost who they were, lost in the city crowd
the city glows, it steals for keep its own
making me a child of two different world &
worry wins only lost trophies

20/10/2021

I walked my way in dream

At crossroad
weather inclement
battering, stormflow
everywhere, once again

at crossroad
weeping, lost in thought
staring at fetish idea of love
as ever-giving non-receiving

of truth, slaughtered at postcodes
of deceits, lies and tradition
the storm heavy now
dark rain falling, killing

I laugh, walk away
seen so much to stay
in this, it is better
I walked my way in dream

20/03/2021

Your backsteps

Let us live
In mind that
Our backsteps
A leftover

Some will leave behind
Backsteps, hurting and regrettable
Too fearful to behold

For others
Sliver, a thing of joy
Worthy to behold

For you
Should it be a fouled air
Remembered with tears

Off it goes

The morning wakes up with darkness
The day promises no dream, no smile
But out the legs go in want of dreams
Quest of its own sun, and sunshine

At the market square
A tsetse fly in a feast
On my naked scrotum, aimlessly
I look, not in want

Of a weapon of destruction, I look
For that of dialogue, more fruit now than ever.
At a time for peace to smile, even
At the altar of slaughter of hate

I spoke
I plead
And off, it goes.

13/11/2021

Mathematics must be there

I want to be a doctor
To help heal the sick
& The college said
Mathematics must be there
Anyhow must I add or minus
Sickness for mathematics to be there

I want to be an engineer
To build structures in the fatherland
& The college said mathematics must be there
Anyhow am I to count numbers of sand
To build for mathematics to be there

I then look on to the business class
To sell and bring in more money
& The college said, too
Mathematics must be there
Am I to count one plus two?
To convince them to buy

For mathematics to be there

Each step taken
The answer same
Mathematics must be there
Mathematics that is logic
That stands on its heads legs up
& The college echoes mathematics must be there

The Breeze

Then came the breeze
Sweet breeze, blowing across
Signifying another season of births
Of the off-the-heat wet season
Across the land

But this sky
Too pregnant to be feared
Heavy over the days and night
No birth, of great concern
While we wait in the usual blame game.

05/06/2021

The season

Another season of dryness
Came unexpected, after the bloom
Across the road so full of marigold flowers, dusty
The harmattan arrived, blooming
With dryness and dusty road

But the rains are off road
For now, and our own hot summer
With cold bayonets of wintry nights
Raging sun heat burns the day
The fields so full of love and flowers

Harmattan comes at festival's time
Thou with dust and heat
& Celebration of the virgin birth
Toasting at the glint of festive
Not for too long, the raucous howls

The land is drier
Swollen with more corpses of
Fauna and flora, dried
& The heat flows on, cursing the day
Leaving behind lava & prayer for another rebirth

The ocean

What a watery beauty
Patience in move
Presence
So full
Of waters
Full of lives
Aquatic

Tell me
What hold
Your lives
Tell me
Of your flowing flowery
Presence across days and nights

Tell me
Of your story
Your beauty
Buried deep
Down o' ocean

Black Friday deals

forget the past
and history
just go for the discount
as in the days of slavery
the black Friday profits

just as they had waited
for discounts and profits, trading
in blood and sweats of blacks
in their black Fridays' deals, so
today Chinese and Indians too
trade in our sweats, milk our bloods
from mirages of discounts at
today's black Friday deals

go to the shows, go to shops
ten percent discounts
fifty percent discounts
twenty percent discounts
even after undisclosed rise
of prices for their profits

indexed. it's a black Friday deal!

Dear brothers

He steals among the church-yard's
Grisly hand
Charlotte Dacre

was Christianity not supposed
to be a gift from God, as
we're told. today's denomination
commercialized. trading in the father's house.
sweat coated profit laden. the pastor's kingdom
here on earth. the worshippers lost in dreams.
exploited. feed them the food of fear, constantly.
of hatred. damnation. picture of hell. And the men
of God cruises to their banks across the city. The banks
give them loan to survive

brother envy not the pagan ministers
parading across the land from their pulpits
those who tear the pockets of followers for profits
building mansions of gold and promising their believers
of theirs in the hereafter. blame them not. blame our clime.
they like us are products of failed conscience.

let them continue in their gold digging
let the rooster continue in its cry
at the middle of the night
for its written that at the end
men will walk with their hands
feed themselves with their legs

Let's save the earth

The bird came for a visit
So sudden, before I notice
Its presence, how seldom
Irresistible. Beautiful. Charming.
The bird rends its songs in velvet tune

Me and the bird in two different worlds apart
Its presence a welcoming tonic to mine
Taking away for awhile thoughts of lost, of pains
Of dreams not dreamt fully, goals not met
As desires faltered away from sight –
The bird and me, in exchange of thoughts, as we exist

Its presence stole my now in exchange of its voice
What another living presence can do for another –
It can change now, change our pains to our peace
So let's save this earth, let us save the fauna and flora
Let's save this beauty
Let's save the earth, save our lives

Tower of Babel

How better can we describe?
This nation of brother going after
Brother's throat? Banditry.
Kidnapping. Rape. Rituals. Human blood
Flowing off in waste. Clotted under the sun
In wait of delayed rains to wash away the pains

We speak in scattered tongues
Like chaff in a stray wind.
Our support or against depend on
Where we come from, blood there
Blood here has different colours.
Its colour is determined by tribe.
Tribal blood group. The wasted blood
Coloured as yoruba, igbo, hausa or what
Not of concern for those with other tribal blood.

We live indeed in a great country
Our country a tower of Babel.

Ghost

The fluttering voices
become the poem of love,
dreams of the dead coming to visit
in songs and wind.

At last you stay
full awake,
till the night silently walks away
in the wind.

vaccination is not enough

the next ever constant
repeating and repeating
cyclical, same as in moonwalk
a new variant found
borders closed, travel bans
WHO warns that vaccination
is key to fight the virus
WHO warns again, vaccination is not enough
wear your masks
maintain social distance
if possible live isolated
WHO warns more vaccination needed-
the boaster- take the boast
back home, song not different
federal government warns
workers not vaccinated should not
be allowed entry to their office,
show your vaccination card and enter your office
what is this all about?
has this pandemic no end
even with this number of deaths

if vaccination is not enough
and prayer too not enough
then what is enough, then this
sit at home, isolate yourself,
avoid crowds, my neighbours
become an island, so strange as fiction
interesting indeed. this world has gotten
more than it could chew. just an atom of disease
giving all sleepless nights. a level of the rich

and poor just as death. all lives lived in fear
and vaccination is not enough and
borders closed, opened to be reclosed.

just amazingly

this hibiscus flower
flowering in the morning
beautiful. dead in dusk
pathetic. pink slacks. it fell

down to manure its plant
a loss turning to a gain.
lost flower, gained nutrient
o' this nature, of unexplainable events

so when the time rolled around
stand up to it, pick up your
laughter. shut down the door of dark specks
off you go. just amazingly.

???

the next teardrop
morning calisthenics …
before the next teardrop

too cold down there
oh sweetheart, be my little synonym

be the subject and object of my dream
perhaps the wrong reason I fall in love

with a stranger
soxna, a stranger at this smiling coast

perhaps it is unavoidable to fall
in love with a wrong person and at wrong place

I leaned over the stranger tree
lost in thought, staring at her ghost

excited of thought of her
before next teardrop

Vague

vague
just a mirage
I stared at vague air,
lost in want of you, transfigured
you emerged, visible, real, androgynous
with those huge brown eyes of yours
stepping out for a hug, a mirage you became

you melted out like under the sun
just like a caveman
leaving the fire stand
to hunt in the dark cold

tremble

suffering. drowning. chasing rainbow wings
with this lean lengthening shadows, of life

as swishing sound strikes
out, the stream screaming in lush

this hopeful world
so full of hopelessness and dreams

swimming in stream of dreams
and of wants, I squeezed in between strange bodies

like the very cup of trembling*
I woke up standing like Jerusalem

see Isaiah 15.17, 22-23

Primordial time

it is being moon
moments the afternoon and evening
hang balanced in mid-haven
the sun in golden flank
the sky smiles its way in
basking in crystal clear light
man and shadow melted in unison

the sun will set
for the moon to rise, to
reign, rule the earth in harmonic shine
till the pneumonic dawn, at harmattan season
all in cold, all of a sudden … the bats of night
dance round the night in want of food

under the thatched roofed parapet
a granny sat, with delicate throat
recounts tales of the moonlight
tales of tortoise, bat and ghost
and the joys of the urchins knew no border
and the old tired man and his snuff
sat, silent of the moon
as he chats online with his ancestors
in our divination technology

African woman

like what we see in the painted poster
you shine in black, beauty in motion
your face so full of hope even in face of pains
though sadness abounds
you run your day with your sledgehammer
to crush events that could hold your dream hostage.
move on. move on & on o'black angel of beauty
let speak of your beauty to the world

move on. look up, there is no better beauty
as you, I know
for your beauty dances naked before all
you are a wondrous woman, an African queen
let your colour proudly speak for you.

The open arm

the day woke up in dreams
whirling, in a red haze
moonlike, as in a full moon
he stood, lost in the wind, of
another day's demand

he walked into space, into the wind
into the end of a grape vine shade
over a ravine, swinging like a boy
in the swing, in a prolonged instant
of mesmerized gravity

he became weightless in life motion
down with sagging steps from hunger,
of hunger, a grove of locust feasts
in his stomach. he still moves on
still lost in an open arm for desire…

The year is winding up

hot and dusty
strong winds of the Sahara
blew across the street

the year is winding up
its long trek for cold
sweet breeze to dusty hot air

hello all, young and old
the harmattan is here
reminding us of our dying year.

14/12/2021

a cosy season

dusty
harsh winds
brown dusty roads
its season
to be cosy
the year pack up
its luggage to leave
winding up in dust
at this time of His birth
signs of a new year's birth
new beginning

to wish the year bye
the wild masquerade
out of the ground
in a wild dance display
climbed the palm tree
with bar hand
the year is dying
in this festive time
in this dusty season
a cosy to celebrate, to be.

The season … droplets of death beads

This season … droplets of death beads
Filter into humans' home
And in flashes, the globe became a theatre of fear
A theatre of death

We live in fear, in the soaring appetite of death blowing

The wind continues to blow deadly across
Leaving wrinkled cries
Short of breath to live
Many became still and soon to go, and forgotten
But the stubborn wind refuses to fade away

We live in fear, in the soaring appetite of death blowing

Mankind will rise again
We will rise again
We will rise again
Mankind will rise again

02/04/20

The coronavirus war

The war splashes on and on
Like a downpour of rain
It spreads, spreading death across

02/04/20

They pay this price for our lives

Wild wild wind across the land
Brutal, smacking, violent
Sounds of fury, gunfires
Flying across like the wild wind

We become primitive men again
As prime-age men vanishing
This is war, not peace
Our substitutes: the soldiers, our warriors

They march, and march on
Like a snail, focused, progressing,
As they crawl, some drop on the wayside
Dropping along their red bleeds for our peace

Them that fall, dropping at the warfronts
We remember today and always, these valiant
Men, the soldiers paying the ultimate price with their bloods
We doff our caps to your glory, to your courage, to your love for our lives

Remembrance

Even at the face of death
Smartly he dressed, to the war front
Courageously, fear of death he left behind
Marching majestically, soldiering on

These soldiers, something else they are
For our peace, their lives they lay down, bare
Their hopes, expectations, all for a world, where
Peace reign. For peace they bled red

The cyclical trenches built for them by men of violence
Enemies of peace, and they respond, in wasteful red bleeding.
Wasteful red. And prime-age men vanquished, vanishing
In front of wars. Mothers weep for lost sons, lost to evil wars

Fathers bemoaned. Look at children orphaned by war. Soldiers' children.
See wives and husbands widowed. All evil fruits of war.
This is our world. World politicians create wars and soldiers die in them.
An evil world, we live in. Hope politicians carry guns too to fight in warfronts.

The soldiers die in wars. Should we let their memories die too?
Should we let them die? Those soldiers of political misfortunes.
Men and women in uniform, called out of barracks at dawn
To defend the fatherland with pride and joy. Should we let them die?

Never let them die. A duty we owe them. And for those that fell by the wayside

At the battle front, warfronts, our flowers and roses we must lay on their tombs
Our heroes they are, these angels of our peace. Honour and glory we adorn on their neck
Their wayside falls we shall honour. Their Remembrance Day our memorial.
Stampede
In this our landscape a chameleon
Changing self like a rough night

The changes its face
From worse to worst
With each tenant in Aso Rock

As if we are in a conquest
From political bohemians
Who rule without any passion?

Look at our people
From Lagos to Maiduguri
Same tales of woes

See people
Stampeded to early grave
By hunger and wants

How can we struggle
Against these instituted stampedes
And stampeders

All in our hands

Birth of a new day
The tiny bird
Hooked up on a twig
Appreciative of this
Waking up, in the street
In sweet dreams melody
Welcoming the day
Calling us too of the day's task
Thanking the great maker for this day

Ours a day it is
To make or mar
All in our hands

Good

Look good
Feel good
  A good world
    To be …
Good

Movement song

The tight curls of life, have I studied, watching it
Moves in just nature one way of life
Then I pulsed and wait, again and again
When the rain fall from the ground upward
And the River Gambia from back to Senegal
Or my age reversed back ward
And father that early sermon
Of why I should know who I am
Ah father where is now, living just in my dreams
Beyond anger my failure
Forward to move, I also must
Waiting till the time of the pollen fall
without goodbyes.

02/06/18

Good morning birds

Kuku ble kuku, kuku ble kuku
It is morning, and fresh birds' songs
Twitting around that cold early morn
The birds twit and sing, singing and twitting
Melodiously
I walk down to the window, opened it
But could only respond: good morning birds

14/05/18

For lovesake

I traverse the land, the sea and the air
And here am I at the doorstep of your heart
Knocking, as I watch this lone bird perched at the tip of the grass, sad

I have seen the corrosive night kiss of love
And the healing touch, too, of morning love

The lone bird perched at the tip of the leave
With mouthful of morning curses, of dejection
But in wait, waiting for consoling touch of love

Here also am I
Knocking at the door-heart of Venus to open
For it is only the mirror that knows all that it had seen

The bleeding heart is like a sunless day, it has no smile

Yet it's raining outside
Heavy rains and rains out there, and you are in the rain
Dancing in the rain, with sparkling smiles of the sun

And healing winds touch the wings of the lone bird
    perching at the tip of the leave, tip of love
It healed you, and it heals me too

Wake up and love
Fragrant love loves love
With nourishing love for all

Freeing us of wounds of yesteryears gone
Rainbow
stars in their sockets shift
no bird's singsong still
and distressed stone terrace winds
fanning downward and upward

after that heated noon
the rains bathe the sky
and the sky smiles
in appreciation

a rainbow
was born

Oge*
Ihe ndi nkpa nke nkwu
Ma anyi amagi tutu ofuo
Oge, ola edo nke oma
Anyi nile were oge haa otu
Ma anyi anagi eweya out oha
N'aka nwatakiri, oge adigi agwugwu
Ma na aka okenye, oge anagi ezuezu
Maka nkea, were kwa oge me ihe mara nma
I we be kwa akwa na oge na dighi anya
Maka oge nke I tupuru n'ohia   .

Time

So precious to lose
We don't appreciate it so
Time, what a valuable gem
We all have equal time
But differently place values on time
For in the hands of the young, time's limitless
But the elderly, time's not enough
So use your time for the good
So that you don't cry in the future
For the time you had wasted in life.

*Written in my own Igbo language. The English Language version is Time below

flooding

we've prayed for rain, rainfalls
not this death, this destruction
floating across the streets
across the farms like flotsam
everywhere crying for some help

The Wailing Streets

"Poverty anywhere is a threat
to prosperity everywhere"
Adams Oshiomhole, as NLC President

In wandering thought of the day
I wondered of this thistle
Of this red raining, untimely timely
Wetting our angry streets

Look across, of flashes of anger mobbing the streets
See, deafening silence of power
An invocation of angry wailings
Flaring up, across the withered land
Insipidly, this anger of hunger
Willing fanned by the figs of anger into
A rustling flame of destructions

See it glow, growing red as it rains
Under this basking boiling sun
See the young seedlings uprooted before their time
From the nozzles of power, and silence and tales prevails

I wandered off again
Of the rock and its prisoner
The aura of death that oozes therein, mystical
I wondered, do we blame the rock or the prisoner
A voice echoed: don't blame the prisoner, blame the rock
Trust, the sufferings out he can't behold
Through the haze of the rock

Then I wandered back

For
Not from too far away
Stood solidly the solidarity of hunger and anger
And anger flickers like a red halo
But this like others before will also fade away
History it will turn, obligated, leaving behind
A hallow solitary footprint for another again next time.

Nightingale

Sweet melodic bird
immortal in my mind
Songs
sweetly orchestrated in eardrums
at the fragrant bush part behind
whilst silver moon sailing and smiling

The song burst from a tree's hand:
chook, chook, chook...
pio, pioo, pioo, ...
all in a crescendo chucking
of night's notes of mellow
aploms: o' my apotheosis
your voice
rendered me aphasia
wish i, o' wish, wish
i could envelope your songs
in an earthen pot container forever
where when i need it:
those songs of a lover
crying out its heart for more love:
i
itys, itys, itys ...

O' nightingale
sing more songs of love, for
sorrowed smitten souls to mend
whose hopes had been Sapped
but, theirs: persistent love
twinkling, twinkling ever as a star

Harmattan Dawn

Confusing, this dawn again
yes, the day ought to have broken by now
dark traps everywhere
traps hidden in the wet grass
as drops of dew scatter
and glisten the dark

Moment later
the chilled sunlight appears with it –
fresh songs of a new day
and raw yolky sound of birdsongs, everywhere

The dawn is at our feet again
Wake as fast as an antelope
for fear of the day's lion ahead

Dawn

The day crawls to break
As drops of dews scatter the ground with mist
Cold, yet Cockerel struggling to crow
This is dawn, chilling dawn light
Creeps into the room through the window
Of the day, of wet grasses
With traps of hidden
Fear of the new day walking into dusk

Wake up, I heard, it is morning
Stinging pains of dawn sting on me
As fresh silence strikes me at the face
Thank God it's dawn, Good morning dawn
So says the raw sounds of birdsongs
As I struggle to face the day today.

2005

Your card arrived

The flowerily card arrived
With lipstick marks
Telegraphing your roly-poly
Arousing thoughts, shared thoughts
with you
Moonlighting together
The hibiscus drawn card, red like rose
Arrived like a thief

It brings with it surprises, of silent seeking
In this unexpected time, just like
A cream creaming against jagged cracks
With its bleaching effects on our stained spot

An escape from

at times we have to
leave the pay-seat of boredom
escape from ourselves for a while

just to the beach I dashed
leaving behind the thorns of work,
the pages of work to attend

sitting on the pay-seat
I stopped listening to music
and only to the corrosive voice of mine

here at the beach, all alone, I sat
as gust of wind slammed my face
with a clap of sound, and of peace

carefully I listen and listen
to the sweet sounds of drifting sand
I listen to the tiny whispering wind
in the dunes' grasses

oh how it feels to be on your own
free, in sweet presence of nature
just away from the pay-seat

Half of the yellow sun

The sun rises
and set at dawn
it dimmed across
these depleted bunkers of mind
and it rises again

half a yellow sun
at dawn
in the minds of urchins
who did not witness the last
half a yellow sun
with its score strife effects

the quest for half a yellow sun
this time around, the aftermath of
a mapped agenda from unlearnt lesson of history

The melt down

Another dusk, economic dusk,
Brother here we are again,
The locusts come visiting,
In the midst of a market meltdown.

A time like this,
Is not a time for blame games,

A time like this,
Requires tons of courage.

Brother!
Set aside your pride, roll up your sleeves,

This labour will be faced by all,
Convict or not.

Frustrated people

Swampy life,
After a barren afternoon,
Life went grey,
Its penis amputated,
By this gibbering society.

Frustrated lot,
Dressed in sorrow and self-pity,
Wait at the roadside,
For hope to stop by,
As the sun, drunk with tears and sweats
Staggers home.

As we wait,
for this hope that will never stop by
I recall the Lord's prayer,
Mumbled 'Give us this day,
Our daily bread', as dusk
Spread its shadow, over our dreams.

Walking away from bygone of you

Adventures in the wild wind life
As I walked my shadow down the lonely road,
A blackbird, perching on the tendrils of
A garden lilac, sang a tune for one.
Dusk hung around the valley,
Rehearsing verses of silence.

-
Yes, like Simeon
I too have seen the Lord
And I wait at the dawn gate of my fortune …
There're good fortunes
Indeed, at dawn.
I walked forward silently
Over any hill, mountain and valley
Forward in silence walk I
Away from these bygone
Adventures of a youth

Economic meltdown

The owl is out in the market
Swarm of locusts everywhere
The market has burnt down
To ashes and loud cries of hunger
In mentholated dusting powdered pains.

With the rest, I staggered along
As the delusive gravitating scorn
Of scorn of singsongs aloud abound
From all official quarters

I, too have seen, the night breaking
Into the full, fresh fragrant morning
And the night of doom over

Yes, not under this present regime
But I know, my pain has an end

For a new dawn

As night gives
Way to morning
The chrysalis
A butterfly
My dream dawns
To great things
Who knows?

This chrysalis
At break of morning
A new hope beginning

My dawn, my dream
My chrysalis, my butterfly

It is a new day, a new hope to behold.

Umunama

Give me my homeland's lakes and streams;
Her many charms display
Before my homesick, lonesome eyes
When I am away
Evelyn Preston Mclean
Not that I would love not to live in you
because of the darkness, the red sandy rough roads,
the screams of insects and crickets;
sights of old women laboring
with heavy basketful
sights of stalls, shops, kiosks –
the Orieukwu coming to life only at evening fall.
Groans of hunger, and tattered children; yes,
quick reference to our dreamed differed rural setting.

Yet I love you, Umunama
I love your fireflies
littering nightfall as starry phantasm
I love your moonlight children's songs,
yet familiar with our jungle-cities' urchins in my abode
I love your care-for-one-another lifestyle
I love the landscapes, Ala'ku's rickety landscape
of our myth-lore riverbed without water;
but valleys unerected as peaks
like a granny burst
I love you, woman
to you, I'd come after this prodigal flight
for spiritual refurbishment

1990

Together as sky

our views differ …

as the sun from the moon
but the linearity of love
and desire solves the quadratic equation

we are like the Niger and Benue
always separately on a move
meeting at a confluence

come love, come
for our correlation coefficient
of our linear existence is love

just as that of moon and stars …

we'll then be together
me and you
you and me
together as one

Poem of dawn at dawn

the morning star still shines
and the earth dims
as men strip to their beddings
like a swarm of tired bees

dawn
time of mind's harvest
when head is still fresh
when head still fresh
from restive sleep
while men of underworld operate
under darkness cover

I write this poem of dawn
at dawn
before the strips of the sky
'd fall on me from high
With the day's burning effect

Rejection

it
may come
in different cloths

it may come
like a dream
half dreamt

it may come
live a dove descending
with darkly news

like a gale of fire
heating the house and its hold
it may come

in the song
unsung
it may come like fierce
wild wind, not to be
grasped or weighed

rejection enwombed
in dreams
never dreamt

rejection in everyday existence
and by you, it is
that pain in me which never
hurt my soul

Mmap New African Poets Series

If you have enjoyed *Like The Starry Night Sky*, consider these other fine books in the **Mmap New African Poets Series** from *Mwanaka Media and Publishing:*

I Threw a Star in a Wine Glass by Fethi Sassi
Best New African Poets 2017 Anthology by Tendai R Mwanaka and Daniel Da Purificacao
Logbook Written by a Drifter by Tendai Rinos Mwanaka
Mad Bob Republic: Bloodlines, Bile and a Crying Child by Tendai Rinos Mwanaka
Zimbolicious Poetry Vol 1 by Tendai R Mwanaka and Edward Dzonze
Zimbolicious Poetry Vol 2 by Tendai R Mwanaka and Edward Dzonze
Zimbolicious: An Anthology of Zimbabwean Literature and Arts, Vol 3 by Tendai Mwanaka
Under The Steel Yoke by Jabulani Mzinyathi
Fly in a Beehive by Thato Tshukudu
Bounding for Light by Richard Mbuthia
Sentiments by Jackson Matimba
Best New African Poets 2018 Anthology by Tendai R Mwanaka and Nsah Mala
Words That Matter by Gerry Sikazwe
The Ungendered by Delia Watterson
Ghetto Symphony by Mandla Mavolwane
Sky for a Foreign Bird by Fethi Sassi
A Portrait of Defiance by Tendai Rinos Mwanaka
Zimbolicious: An Anthology of Zimbabwean Literature and Arts, Vol 4 by Tendai Mwanaka and Jabulani Mzinyathi
When Escape Becomes the only Lover by Tendai R Mwanaka
ويَسهَرُ اللَّيلُ عَلَى شَفَتي...وَالغَمَام by Fethi Sassi

A Letter to the President by Mbizo Chirasha
This is not a poem by Richard Inya
Pressed flowers by John Eppel
Righteous Indignation by Jabulani Mzinyathi:
Blooming Cactus by Mikateko Mbambo
Rhythm of Life by Olivia Ngozi Osouha
Travellers Gather Dust and Lust by Gabriel Awuah Mainoo
Chitungwiza Mushamukuru: An Anthology from Zimbabwe's Biggest Ghetto Town by Tendai Rinos Mwanaka
Zimbolicious: An Anthology of Zimbabwean Literature and Arts, Vol 5 by Tendai Mwanaka
Because Sadness is Beautiful? by Tanaka Chidora
Of Fresh Bloom and Smoke by Abigail George
Shades of Black by Edward Dzonze
Best New African Poets 2020 Anthology by Tendai Rinos Mwanaka, Lorna Telma Zita and Balddine Moussa
This Body is an Empty Vessel by Beaton Galafa
Between Places by Tendai Rinos Mwanaka
Best New African Poets 2021 Anthology by Tendai Rinos Mwanaka, Lorna Telma Zita and Balddine Moussa
Zimbolicious: An Anthology of Zimbabwean Literature and Arts, Vol 6 by Tendai Mwanaka and Chenjerai Mhondera
A Matter of Inclusion by Chad Norman
Keeping the Sun Secret by Mariel Awendit
سِجلٌ مَكتُوبٌ لتَائه □ by Tendai Rinos Mwanaka
Ghetto Blues by Tendai Rinos Mwanaka
Zimbolicious: An Anthology of Zimbabwean Literature and Arts, Vol 7 by Tendai Rinos Mwanaka and Tanaka Chidora
Best New African Poets 2022 Anthology by Tendai Rinos Mwanaka and Helder Simbad
Dark Lines of History by Sithembele Isaac Xhegwana
a sky is falling by Nica Cornell

Death of a Statue by Samuel Chuma
Along the way by Jabulani Mzinyathi
Strides of Hope by Tawanda Chigavazira
Young Galaxies by Abigail George
Coming of Age by Gift Sakirai
Mother's Kitchen and Other Places by Antreka. M. Tladi
Best New African Poets 2023 Anthology by Tendai Rinos Mwanaka, Helder Simbad and Gerald Mpesse
Zimbolicious Anthology Vol 8 by Tendai Rinos Mwanaka and Mathew T Chikono
Broken Maps by Riak Marial Riak
Formless by Raïs Neza Boneza
Of poets, gods, ghosts. Irritants and storytellers by Tendai Rinos Mwanaka
Ethiopian Aliens by Clersidia Nzorozwa
In The Inferno by Jabulani Mzinyathi
Who Told You To Be God by Mariel Awendit
Nobody Loves Me by Abigail
The Stories of Stories by Nkwazi Mhango
Nhorido by Siphosami Ndlovu and Tinashe Chikumbo
Best New African Poets 10th Anniversary: Selected English African Poets by Tendai Rinos Mwanaka
Best New African Poets 10th Anniversary: Interviews and Reviews of African Poets by Tendai Rinos Mwanaka
Best New African Poets 10th Anniversary: African Languages and Collaborations by   Tendai Rinos Mwanaka
ANTOLOGIA DOS MELHORES "NOVOS" POETAS AFRICANOS 10° Aniversário: Poetas Africanos Da Língua Portuguesa Selecionados by Lorna Telma Zita and Tendai Rinos Mwanaka
ABRACADABRA, by Olivia Ngozi Osuoha
DES MEILLEURS "NOUVEAUX" POÈTES AFRICAINS 10ᵉ Anniversaire : Poètes africains d'expression française by Geraldin Mpesse and Tendai Rinos Mwanaka
Taurai Amai by Cosmas Tasvika Manhanhanha

Nhemeramutupo by Oscar Gwiriri
Ntombentle: Selected Poems by Sithembele Isaac Xhegwana
African Poetry Anthology: Chapbooks, Vol 1 by Tendai Rinos Mwanaka, Lorna Telma Zita and Helder Simbad
Juices Of The Forbidden Fruit by Tapuwa Tremor, Mapaike

www.ingramcontent.com/pod-product-compliance
Lightning Source LLC
Chambersburg PA
CBHW071006160426
43193CB00012B/1941